MANIFEST that Shit!

Positive Thoughts + Positive Emotions = Positive Outcomes

$1,000,000 in sales!

@sweetcookiewash

Sweet Cookie Jar LLC
6791 NW 25th Ct Sunrise, FL 33313
sweetcookies.org

MANIFEST that Shit!

Nobody will believe in you if you don't believe in you

Success is like fasting. If you were raised in a religious household, you are familiar with the practice of fasting, which is a period of abstinence from food or drink, to remain focused on spiritual growth in service to God. You sacrifice two of the most vital things in life to offer praises to God and to receive an abundance of blessings in return. Success commands the same reverence and discipline. Just like in fasting, you must make sacrifices in life to achieve success. You have to be honest about the habits, people, things, and even locations that you know you need to give up to reach your goals! And of course, like most things in life that are good for you, letting go is hard, but how much more are you willing to lose while holding on?

When you let go, in most cases you are losing:

1. A toxic, unhappy, abusive, boring relationship

2. Unmotivated, unsupportive, hateful fake friends

3. A city of people that do not support you

4. Clubs that make you waste money

5. Spending habits that do not grow your wealth

6. Drugs or activities that make you unproductive

Since you're on a roll, go ahead and also let go of negative thoughts, beliefs, and practices. The law of attraction is working all the time. It is not a button that you can turn on and off. The things that you say, think, and do are manifested into your life accordingly. If you launch a business and sales are slow or nonexistent in the first two months and you begin to think " this isn' t working out very well;" you can bet that things will "not work out very well" for your business no matter how much you post or promote. It doesn't matter how much effort you put behind a goal; if you don't believe it will be successful, it won't. Having faith that things ARE working out, even if they are not working the way you expected, is key. If you notice, I did not say have faith that things "will" or "will soon," get better. Instead, I firmly reassured you that you must be confidently rooted in your belief that things are currently excellent to attract more excellent things in your life. The same applies to misfortune. If you say you are having a bad day, more bad things will continue to happen because you have already claimed it. First, you run late, then you spill something on yourself, and the streak of misfortune continues for as long as you continue to claim it.

Manifest That Shit!

And no, you don't have to physically utter the words out of your mouth to seal your faith because the universe responds to your energy which means, if you are thinking negative thoughts, they will manifest into your life. You either release positive energy or negative energy; there is no in-between. If you have a negative outlook on things in your life such as business, relationships, and even love, that negativity will signal the universe to return negative energy into your life and in multitudes. Always monitor your thoughts and not just your words. The things that you manifest in your life is a direct reflection of the thoughts that you harbor inside your mind. Negative thoughts come in different shapes and forms. Even if you say, "I am not negative," on some deeper level, your energy is piggybacking on a negative thought. Instead, practice saying "I am positive." How did that sound and feel?

Apply this to all areas of your life. Resist the urge to focus on what you lack and adopt a razor-sharp focus on what you have or what you want to have. If you want support, give support and show gratitude to those who support you. When you do this, the universe (and the people who you support), will pay you back in kind. Do not waste any more time or energy focusing on the support that you are not receiving. Those thoughts and people will drain you. Do not waste any more time or energy dwelling on the unpleasant aspects of your life, even those aspects that you just simply cannot avoid, such as your place of employment. If your job makes you unhappy or is filled with drama, positive thinking will not change the unhealthiness of that environment or cause you to like the place any more than you do currently. However, thinking, saying, and writing about the kind of happiness that you desire from the place where you work will allow the universe to open up job opportunities at that ideal place. And make no mistake, the universe cannot deliver that ideal place, position, or job to you if you do not put in heavy work to manifest it. Nothing will ever just fall into your lap unless you put effort into manifesting it. And so, the first thing you need to do to receive what you want (and desire), is to take action! In the case of your ideal job, send a resume, and then go by the building where the job is and imagine yourself walking into the building for work. On another day, go there in the evening and envision yourself walking out with the crowd after work. Better yet, go inside the building and wait for the crowd to come out and walk out with them. If you are ready to take yourself seriously, go as far as picking out the new outfit that you will wear to work at that ideal place on your first day. Submit yourself to positive thinking and Manifest That Shit!

Never Let The Fear of Falling Keep You from Running !

Now that you've let go of the toxic things in your life, let's get started! I started my business with absolutely no support. Just imagine me telling my family that although I have a bachelor's degree, I am putting it aside to act on YouTube, make vagina products, and sell coconut water on the side of the road. I'm sure you can imagine the level of skepticism that followed that announcement, but I remained focused and stayed confident. I was excited to have the option of failing because that meant I had the opportunity for success. You must be willing to fail to achieve success. Achieving greatness requires lessons learned, and you can only learn from trial and error. Do not be afraid to try, fail, and try again. Set clear goals and work without fear!

This year I am making: _____

Next year I am making: _____

In 5 years I am making: _____

Good job! In 2017, I had $0 when I wrote that I would make $100,000 in sales. By the end of the year, I surpassed that goal, making $107,219 in revenue. The next year (2018), I put it out into the universe that I would double that amount, but instead, I quadrupled that amount and made $400,000 that year. When 2019 started, my soul was set on fire! I had unlocked the power to manifest my goals into my life and I wanted to see what would happen if I aimed for bigger goals. At the beginning of 2019, I decided that I am going to make $1 million in online sales, and I hit that goal on Friday, November 29, 2019. Before hitting that goal on the 29th, I had taken a photograph on November 15th holding up one finger to signify $1 million in sales, and I meditated on that picture (and my goal) every single day until I reached the $1million mark. Whether you have a physical business, an online store or you offer a type of service, set goals for your business and locations. If you are in business and also work a 9 to 5, do not mix the income from your job with the income from your business. Set separate and specific goals for your business only.

It's Just Numbers!

Ex. If you plan to make 50,0000 this year, break it down into daily, weekly, and monthly goals.

Daily	Weekly	Monthly
$136.98	$961.53	$4,166

It's Already Yours!

— Universe

Manifest That Shit!

Manifesting My Home

Circle One:

The home I want to get this year is a(n):

Apartment   Condo

House   Townhouse

Im already living in the house I want this year

I Desire:

Bedrooms:_____

Bathrooms:_____

Country/City/Town/State:_____

Write any special rooms, features, amenities or colors it will have:

_____

_____

_____

_____

_____

Manifesting My Home

<u>Circle One:</u>

The dream home is a:

Villa   Condo

House   Townhouse

Im already living in my dream home

I Desire:

Bedrooms:_____

Bathrooms:_____

Country/City/Town/State:_____

<u>**Write any special rooms, features, amenities or colors it will have:**</u>

_____

_____

_____

_____

_____

Manifest That Shit!

Manifesting My Home

What car(s) are you buying and when?

Example:

Mercedes Benz: November 2021

_____

_____

_____

Any special details about the car(s)/ truck(s)? Ex. Color , rims, interior etc.?

_____

_____

_____

_____

_____

How much does the car(s) cost:

_____

_____

_____

Make sure you know or find out the cost of the car(s)
because you will need to create a savings plan.**

Manifest That Shit!

It's Time to Travel!

What countries or cities will you visit this year? Pick the month you will be going and be specific about your plans. When you begin to manifest your goals, be clear and intentional about those goals. The more specific the goal is the clearer the vision and the path to achieving that goal. Find out when is the best time of the year to go to your dream destination based on factors such as weather and current events. Always aim to get the most fulfilling experience from the trip by doing things that keep you involved in the moment. Remember, these are your goals and they serve a greater purpose. And so, just like every other goal, if you have to accomplish your travel goals on your own and by yourself, use that opportunity to grow and evolve. Family, friends, or even romantic partners should never be a reason you do not accomplish this or any other goal. I have traveled many times, met great people, and had lots of fun - alone!

Example:
1. New Orleans - July
2. Jamaica - December

Your turn!

This year I am going to...

_____

_____

_____

_____

_____

_____

Manifest That Shit!

Manifesting Love & Relationships

This is a funny, yet tricky one because the universe quite literally gives you what you ask for. I remember saying things like, "it's ok if he is a cheater as long as I don't know," or asking for unspecific things such as a rich man, without fully understanding the possible implications behind those lavish features. I neglected to specifically ask for good qualities such as a supportive and respectful partner when in fact, those qualities are worth more than any amount of money. I had created a list of what I wanted in a man but what I learned is that specificity, modesty, and rationality are very important and necessary components that were lacking on my list. Another very important component that should be one everyone's list is the list of nonnegotiables. These are qualities that you will not compromise or negotiate and that you strictly enforce when choosing a partner. And be rational about this. It is very important that you understand that your partner is NOT responsible for making you happy. If you are unhappy or insecure, those are things you should address before entering a relationship. Do not subject your partner to those internal issues. Your partner cannot fix your problems. It is perfectly ok to be attracted to someone who has similar interests and likes as you do. And it is even better when they have a similar drive and similar goals as you do. If you desire a partner who is ready to travel the world, then go travel the world so the universe understands that you mean business! If you want a partner to drink and party with, then hit the club scenes frequently. Put yourself in the position for the things you want to come to fruition. Manifest That Shit!

Non Negotiables:

_____

_____

_____

Manifest That Shit!

Damn baby you make me feel ...

Another key factor in manifesting is to understand the feeling you want to have. For example, some men may say they would like a big booty woman that cooks, rubs his back, and respects him because it makes him feel like a king; while some women may say they want a tall, rich, sexy man who is very well endowed, takes her on dates and pay her bills because that makes her feel loved. Manifestation can occur based on the feeling that you want to create in your life. For example, happiness is a state of mind, but it is also a feeling. It is a feeling of satisfaction and content. Take the time to understand the feeling you want in your life and don't limit yourself based on your current position or your current tax bracket. Most people choose their partner based on how that person made them feel, and their relationship flourishes overtime when that feeling is maintained and nurtured. So, as apart of manifesting love, identity the feeling that you want. If you are already in a relationship, focus on what you want to feel from your partner. Meditate on it. If the feeling is not there currently, but there is something else that you love about your partner or your relationship, meditate on the feeling you want with razor-sharp focus and watch it be manifested within your relationship.

Possible reasons a man would want a big booty chef that plays video games could be because he wants a relationship where he feels:

1. Sexual Attraction
2. Nurtured
3. Mutual Interests

Damn baby you make me feel ...

Write ten (10) sentences of how your lover makes you feel by the actions they take or the things that you do together. Write the sentences as if this person is already in your life. Use your imagination to create scenarios and brag about your dream man or dream woman!

Examples

" You buy me cookie wash when you see the bottle is low"
(trait: considerate; feeling: cared for and noticed)

"I love how you bring flowers and take me on dates"
(trait: romantic; feeling: loved and appreciated)

"Every time we travel we try new things, get drunk, dance, & meet new people"
(traits: adventurous, fun, & friendly; feeling: excitement)

"I feel safe and financially secure with you"

BRAG ABOUT YOUR LOVER !

"Where will I go to meet a lover that enjoys the same things as me"

_____

_____

_____

What feeling?

1. _____
2. _____
3. _____
4. _____
5. _____
6. _____
7. _____
8. _____
9. _____
10. _____

Manifest That Shit!

The writing strategy that I introduced for your love life can be applied to every area in your life! I want you to use the power of thinking it, writing it, saying it, & putting it into action to create the life you want. The law of attraction gives you what you focus on, so it is important to visualize and write about your success!

You can get started with thinking of three (3) things:

1. How do you want to make your customers feel?

2. How will you promote to customers?

3. What are your expansion plans and how well are they doing?

"When my customers use cookie wash they feel confident, fresh, healthy, & happy that they have a vagina."

"I pass out 50 flyers everyday so my company is well known and supported!"

"My restaurant is always full, my recipe book is on Amazon's best seller list, and my barbecue sauce is flying off the shelves at Walmart!"

Manifest That Shit!

Manifest That Shit!

When you write down the things that you want to happen as if they are already happening, you are welcoming these opportunities in your life. You don't own a restaurant as yet, but when you write down that your restaurant is always full, you are letting success know that it is welcomed in your life. When you claim a full restaurant, your belief and the effort that you put into manifesting positive thoughts and energy will attract a full restaurant to you. Let's say that you are paying $5000 to an Instagram influencer or a billboard company for a promotional ad. Before, during, and after the ad, utilize the power of manifesting by writing out everything that you will accomplish before, during, after, and because of the ad! Write the goals you want to achieve, be descriptive, and visualize how amazing it feels to accomplish them!

Example:

Goal: Promotion with @starrdawkinz

Visualize & Write It

1. I'm excited to have 10,000 new followers

2. I made $10,000 in sales

3. My new customers feel excited to try my lotion

Every time you have a goal that is important to you, manifest it!
After writing it constantly, say it and visualize it!
Ex. Fitness goals, relationships, business, etc.

Visualize

The universe is also a visual learner. It is learning what to give you based on what you are feeding your vision. If you want to travel to Mexico, look at pictures of adventures in Mexico. If you want to open a store, walk into stores and imagine your products on the shelves. If you want to buy a home, go to open houses in the community that you want to live in. Window shopping and test driving are great ways to manifest! When you write about your dream guy or girl, envision yourself being kissed, going on dates, and laughing together. If you want a partner who will drink coffee with you and help you plan things, then bring a notebook to a coffee shop and visualize it! This is how you take action toward your future. If you spend your leisure at home and keep yourself locked into that tiny little box called your reality, you will never find those opportunities to excel. Faith without work is dead.

Let's Break Down The Steps

1. Be willing to let go of negative thoughts, people, habits, or places in your life.

2. *Think it!* Be descriptive about exactly what you want so you can set specific goals.

3. *Write it!* Manifest what you want by writing details, numbers, feelings, etc.

4. *Visualize it!* Look at images, make vision boards, take pictures, videos, or create images in your mind that align with your goals.

5. *Affirm it!* Empower yourself daily by saying positive statements that affirm every goal you have is presently happening.

6. *Plan it!* Get organized and write out the steps you will take to achieve your goal.

7. *Go get it!* Every day do at least one (1) thing that brings you closer to your goal.

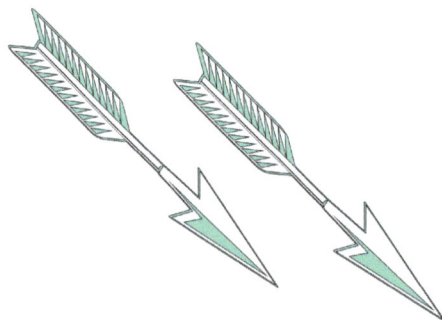

Self Care **GOALS**

SELF CARE GOALS

_____   _____

_____   _____

_____   _____

_____   _____

_____   _____

Now, AFFIRM IT
(Confirm your goals! Talk about them like you KNOW they are true)

Ex. I have no problems, only opportunities _____

Ex. I put myself first and I am filled with joy _____

_____

_____

_____

_____

_____

_____

_____

_____

_____

_____

_____

Turn the page to zoom in on these goals
and _VISUALIZE_ them!

Manifest That Shit!

Self Care GOALS

Ex. My masseuse's hands are so good that I look forward to getting my massage every Wednesday

_____

_____

_____

_____

_____

_____

_____

_____

_____

_____

_____

_____

_____

_____

_____

_____

_____

_____

_____

Manifest That Shit!

Business GOALS

BUSINESS GOALS

_____   _____

_____   _____

_____   _____

_____   _____

_____   _____

Now, AFFIRM IT

(Confirm your goals! Talk about them like you KNOW they are true)

Ex. My business is successful

Ex. Money flows easily to me

_____

_____

_____

_____

_____

_____

_____

_____

_____

_____

_____

_____

Turn the page to zoom in on these goals
and _VISUALIZE_ them!

Manifest That Shit!

Business GOALS

VISUALIZE & WRITE IT

(Bring these goals to life! Write the things you are visualizing about the goal(s))

Ex. Chris Brown reposted my t-shirt and I'm getting 100 orders per minute

_____

_____

_____

_____

_____

_____

_____

_____

_____

_____

_____

_____

_____

_____

_____

_____

_____

Manifest That Shit!

Relationship GOALS

RELATIONSHIP GOALS

_____   _____

_____   _____

_____   _____

_____   _____

_____   _____

Now, AFFIRM IT

(Confirm your goals! Talk about them like you KNOW they are true)

Ex. My relationship is filled with love, respect and stability _____

Ex. I am worthy of love so I only attract affectionate partners _____

_____

_____

_____

_____

_____

_____

_____

_____

_____

_____

_____

Turn the page to zoom in on these goals
and *VISUALIZE* them!

Manifest That Shit!

Relationship GOALS

Ex. I love how you hold my hand while we walk on the beach.

_____

_____

_____

_____

_____

_____

_____

_____

_____

_____

_____

_____

_____

_____

_____

_____

_____

_____

Manifest That Shit!

GOALS

_____

_____ GOALS

_____   _____

_____   _____

_____   _____

_____   _____

_____   _____

Now, AFFIRM IT

_____

_____

_____

_____

_____

_____

_____

_____

_____

_____

_____

_____

_____

Turn the page to zoom in on these goals
and *VISUALIZE* them!

Manifest That Shit!

VISUALIZE & WRITE IT

Manifest That Shit!

GOALS

_____

_____ GOALS

_____
_____
_____
_____
_____
_____
_____
_____

Now, AFFIRM IT

_____
_____
_____
_____
_____
_____
_____
_____
_____
_____
_____
_____
_____
_____
_____
_____

Turn the page to zoom in on these goals
and *VISUALIZE* them!

Manifest That Shit!

GOALS

VISUALIZE & WRITE IT

Manifest That Shit!

GOALS

_____

_____ GOALS

_____ _____
_____ _____
_____ _____
_____ _____
_____ _____

Now, AFFIRM IT

_____
_____
_____
_____
_____
_____
_____
_____
_____
_____
_____
_____
_____

Turn the page to zoom in on these goals
and _VISUALIZE_ them!

Manifest That Shit!

GOALS

Manifest That Shit!

GOALS

_____

_____ GOALS

_____   _____

_____   _____

_____   _____

_____   _____

_____   _____

Now, AFFIRM IT

_____

_____

_____

_____

_____

_____

_____

_____

_____

_____

_____

_____

_____

_____

Turn the page to zoom in on these goals
and _VISUALIZE_ them!

Manifest That Shit!

GOALS

VISUALIZE & WRITE IT

_____

_____

_____

_____

_____

_____

_____

_____

_____

_____

_____

_____

_____

_____

_____

_____

_____

_____

Manifest That Shit!

GOALS

_____

_____ GOALS

_____ _____

_____ _____

_____ _____

_____ _____

_____ _____

Now, AFFIRM IT

_____

_____

_____

_____

_____

_____

_____

_____

_____

_____

_____

_____

_____

Turn the page to zoom in on these goals
and *VISUALIZE* them!

Manifest That Shit!

GOALS

VISUALIZE & WRITE IT

Manifest That Shit!

GOALS

_____

_____ GOALS

_____
_____
_____
_____

Now, AFFIRM IT

_____
_____
_____
_____
_____
_____
_____
_____
_____
_____
_____
_____
_____

Turn the page to zoom in on these goals
and *VISUALIZE* them!

Manifest That Shit!

GOALS

VISUALIZE & WRITE IT

Manifest That Shit!

My formula is simple. Set yearly goals, then break those
goals down into months, then into weeks, and finally, break them down into days.

January TO DO LIST ✓

WEEK 1:

_____

_____

_____

_____

_____

_____

_____

_____

_____

End of week *checkoff!* *How much did I accomplish this week?*

GOAL 1 ☐ GOAL 2 ☐ GOAL 3 ☐ GOAL 4 ☐ GOAL 5 ☐

WEEK 2:

_____

_____

_____

_____

_____

_____

_____

_____

_____

End of week *checkoff!* *How much did I accomplish this week?*

GOAL 1 ☐ GOAL 2 ☐ GOAL 3 ☐ GOAL 4 ☐ GOAL 5 ☐

Manifest That Shit!

January TO DO LIST ✓

WEEK 3:

_____

_____

_____

_____

_____

_____

_____

_____

_____

End of week *checkoff*! How much did I accomplish this week?

GOAL 1 ☐ GOAL 2 ☐ GOAL 3 ☐ GOAL 4 ☐ GOAL 5 ☐

WEEK 4:

_____

_____

_____

_____

_____

_____

_____

_____

_____

End of week *checkoff*! How much did I accomplish this week?

GOAL 1 ☐ GOAL 2 ☐ GOAL 3 ☐ GOAL 4 ☐ GOAL 5 ☐

February TO DO LIST ✔

WEEK 1:

_____

_____

_____

_____

_____

_____

_____

_____

_____

End of week checkoff! How much did I accomplish this week?

GOAL 1 ☐ GOAL 2 ☐ GOAL 3 ☐ GOAL 4 ☐ GOAL 5 ☐

WEEK 2:

_____

_____

_____

_____

_____

_____

_____

_____

_____

End of week checkoff! How much did I accomplish this week?

GOAL 1 ☐ GOAL 2 ☐ GOAL 3 ☐ GOAL 4 ☐ GOAL 5 ☐

Manifest That Shit!

February TO DO LIST ✓

WEEK 3:

_____

_____

_____

_____

_____

_____

_____

_____

_____

_____

End of week *checkoff*! How much did I accomplish this week?

GOAL 1 ☐ GOAL 2 ☐ GOAL 3 ☐ GOAL 4 ☐ GOAL 5 ☐

WEEK 4:

_____

_____

_____

_____

_____

_____

_____

_____

_____

_____

End of week *checkoff*! How much did I accomplish this week?

GOAL 1 ☐ GOAL 2 ☐ GOAL 3 ☐ GOAL 4 ☐ GOAL 5 ☐

March To Do List ✓

WEEK 1:

_____

_____

_____

_____

_____

_____

_____

_____

_____

End of week ***checkoff****! How much did I accomplish this week?*

GOAL 1 ☐   GOAL 2 ☐   GOAL 3 ☐   GOAL 4 ☐   GOAL 5 ☐

WEEK 2:

_____

_____

_____

_____

_____

_____

_____

_____

_____

End of week ***checkoff****! How much did I accomplish this week?*

GOAL 1 ☐   GOAL 2 ☐   GOAL 3 ☐   GOAL 4 ☐   GOAL 5 ☐

Manifest That Shit!

March **TO DO LIST** ✓

WEEK 3:

_____

_____

_____

_____

_____

_____

_____

_____

_____

_____

End of week ***checkoff****! How much did I accomplish this week?*

GOAL 1 ☐ GOAL 2 ☐ GOAL 3 ☐ GOAL 4 ☐ GOAL 5 ☐

WEEK 4:

_____

_____

_____

_____

_____

_____

_____

_____

_____

End of week ***checkoff****! How much did I accomplish this week?*

GOAL 1 ☐ GOAL 2 ☐ GOAL 3 ☐ GOAL 4 ☐ GOAL 5 ☐

April TO DO LIST ✓

WEEK 1:

_____

_____

_____

_____

_____

_____

_____

_____

_____

End of week **checkoff**! *How much did I accomplish this week?*

GOAL 1 ☐ GOAL 2 ☐ GOAL 3 ☐ GOAL 4 ☐ GOAL 5 ☐

WEEK 2:

_____

_____

_____

_____

_____

_____

_____

_____

_____

End of week **checkoff**! *How much did I accomplish this week?*

GOAL 1 ☐ GOAL 2 ☐ GOAL 3 ☐ GOAL 4 ☐ GOAL 5 ☐

Manifest That Shit!

April TO DO LIST ✓

WEEK 3:

_____

_____

_____

_____

_____

_____

_____

_____

_____

End of week **checkoff**! *How much did I accomplish this week?*

GOAL 1 ☐ GOAL 2 ☐ GOAL 3 ☐ GOAL 4 ☐ GOAL 5 ☐

WEEK 4:

_____

_____

_____

_____

_____

_____

_____

_____

_____

End of week **checkoff**! *How much did I accomplish this week?*

GOAL 1 ☐ GOAL 2 ☐ GOAL 3 ☐ GOAL 4 ☐ GOAL 5 ☐

May **TO DO LIST** ✓

WEEK 1:

_____

_____

_____

_____

_____

_____

_____

_____

_____

End of week checkoff! How much did I accomplish this week?

GOAL 1 ☐ GOAL 2 ☐ GOAL 3 ☐ GOAL 4 ☐ GOAL 5 ☐

WEEK 2:

_____

_____

_____

_____

_____

_____

_____

_____

_____

End of week checkoff! How much did I accomplish this week?

GOAL 1 ☐ GOAL 2 ☐ GOAL 3 ☐ GOAL 4 ☐ GOAL 5 ☐

Manifest That Shit!

May TO DO LIST ✔

WEEK 3:

_____

_____

_____

_____

_____

_____

_____

_____

_____

_____

End of week **checkoff**! *How much did I accomplish this week?*

GOAL 1 ☐   GOAL 2 ☐   GOAL 3 ☐   GOAL 4 ☐   GOAL 5 ☐

WEEK 4:

_____

_____

_____

_____

_____

_____

_____

_____

_____

End of week **checkoff**! *How much did I accomplish this week?*

GOAL 1 ☐   GOAL 2 ☐   GOAL 3 ☐   GOAL 4 ☐   GOAL 5 ☐

June TO DO LIST ✓

WEEK 1:

_____

_____

_____

_____

_____

_____

_____

_____

_____

End of week **checkoff***! How much did I accomplish this week?*
GOAL 1 ☐ GOAL 2 ☐ GOAL 3 ☐ GOAL 4 ☐ GOAL 5 ☐

WEEK 2:

_____

_____

_____

_____

_____

_____

_____

_____

_____

End of week **checkoff***! How much did I accomplish this week?*
GOAL 1 ☐ GOAL 2 ☐ GOAL 3 ☐ GOAL 4 ☐ GOAL 5 ☐

Manifest That Shit!

June **TO DO LIST** ✓

WEEK 3:

_____
_____
_____
_____
_____
_____
_____
_____
_____
_____

End of week **checkoff**! *How much did I accomplish this week?*

GOAL 1 ☐ GOAL 2 ☐ GOAL 3 ☐ GOAL 4 ☐ GOAL 5 ☐

WEEK 4:

_____
_____
_____
_____
_____
_____
_____
_____
_____
_____

End of week **checkoff**! *How much did I accomplish this week?*

GOAL 1 ☐ GOAL 2 ☐ GOAL 3 ☐ GOAL 4 ☐ GOAL 5 ☐

July TO DO LIST ✔

WEEK 1:

_____

_____

_____

_____

_____

_____

_____

_____

_____

_____

End of week ***checkoff****! How much did I accomplish this week?*

GOAL 1 ☐ GOAL 2 ☐ GOAL 3 ☐ GOAL 4 ☐ GOAL 5 ☐

WEEK 2:

_____

_____

_____

_____

_____

_____

_____

_____

_____

End of week ***checkoff****! How much did I accomplish this week?*

GOAL 1 ☐ GOAL 2 ☐ GOAL 3 ☐ GOAL 4 ☐ GOAL 5 ☐

Manifest That Shit!

July TO DO LIST ✓

WEEK 3:

_____

_____

_____

_____

_____

_____

_____

_____

_____

End of week **checkoff**! *How much did I accomplish this week?*

GOAL 1 ☐ GOAL 2 ☐ GOAL 3 ☐ GOAL 4 ☐ GOAL 5 ☐

WEEK 4:

_____

_____

_____

_____

_____

_____

_____

_____

_____

End of week **checkoff**! *How much did I accomplish this week?*

GOAL 1 ☐ GOAL 2 ☐ GOAL 3 ☐ GOAL 4 ☐ GOAL 5 ☐

August TO DO LIST ✔

WEEK 1:

_____

_____

_____

_____

_____

_____

_____

_____

_____

End of week **checkoff**! *How much did I accomplish this week?*

GOAL 1 ☐ GOAL 2 ☐ GOAL 3 ☐ GOAL 4 ☐ GOAL 5 ☐

WEEK 2:

_____

_____

_____

_____

_____

_____

_____

_____

_____

End of week **checkoff**! *How much did I accomplish this week?*

GOAL 1 ☐ GOAL 2 ☐ GOAL 3 ☐ GOAL 4 ☐ GOAL 5 ☐

Manifest That Shit!

August TO DO LIST ✓

WEEK 3:

_____

_____

_____

_____

_____

_____

_____

_____

_____

_____

End of week **checkoff**! *How much did I accomplish this week?*

GOAL 1 ☐ GOAL 2 ☐ GOAL 3 ☐ GOAL 4 ☐ GOAL 5 ☐

WEEK 4:

_____

_____

_____

_____

_____

_____

_____

_____

_____

_____

End of week **checkoff**! *How much did I accomplish this week?*

GOAL 1 ☐ GOAL 2 ☐ GOAL 3 ☐ GOAL 4 ☐ GOAL 5 ☐

September TO DO LIST ✓

WEEK 1:

_____

_____

_____

_____

_____

_____

_____

_____

_____

End of week checkoff! How much did I accomplish this week?

GOAL 1 ☐   GOAL 2 ☐   GOAL 3 ☐   GOAL 4 ☐   GOAL 5 ☐

WEEK 2:

_____

_____

_____

_____

_____

_____

_____

_____

End of week checkoff! How much did I accomplish this week?

GOAL 1 ☐   GOAL 2 ☐   GOAL 3 ☐   GOAL 4 ☐   GOAL 5 ☐

Manifest That Shit!

September TO DO LIST ✓

WEEK 3:

_____

_____

_____

_____

_____

_____

_____

_____

_____

End of week **checkoff**_! How much did I accomplish this week?_

GOAL 1 ☐   GOAL 2 ☐   GOAL 3 ☐   GOAL 4 ☐   GOAL 5 ☐

WEEK 4:

_____

_____

_____

_____

_____

_____

_____

_____

_____

End of week **checkoff**_! How much did I accomplish this week?_

GOAL 1 ☐   GOAL 2 ☐   GOAL 3 ☐   GOAL 4 ☐   GOAL 5 ☐

October TO DO LIST ✓

WEEK 1:

_____

_____

_____

_____

_____

_____

_____

_____

End of week checkoff! How much did I accomplish this week?

GOAL 1 ☐   GOAL 2 ☐   GOAL 3 ☐   GOAL 4 ☐   GOAL 5 ☐

WEEK 2:

_____

_____

_____

_____

_____

_____

_____

_____

End of week checkoff! How much did I accomplish this week?

GOAL 1 ☐   GOAL 2 ☐   GOAL 3 ☐   GOAL 4 ☐   GOAL 5 ☐

Manifest That Shit!

October TO DO LIST ✓

WEEK 3:

_____

_____

_____

_____

_____

_____

_____

_____

_____

End of week **checkoff.** *How much did I accomplish this week?*

GOAL 1 ☐   GOAL 2 ☐   GOAL 3 ☐   GOAL 4 ☐   GOAL 5 ☐

WEEK 4:

_____

_____

_____

_____

_____

_____

_____

_____

_____

End of week **checkoff.** *How much did I accomplish this week?*

GOAL 1 ☐   GOAL 2 ☐   GOAL 3 ☐   GOAL 4 ☐   GOAL 5 ☐

November TO DO LIST ✔

WEEK 1:

_____
_____
_____
_____
_____
_____
_____
_____

*End of week **checkoff**! How much did I accomplish this week?*
GOAL 1 ☐ GOAL 2 ☐ GOAL 3 ☐ GOAL 4 ☐ GOAL 5 ☐

WEEK 2:

_____
_____
_____
_____
_____
_____
_____
_____

*End of week **checkoff**! How much did I accomplish this week?*
GOAL 1 ☐ GOAL 2 ☐ GOAL 3 ☐ GOAL 4 ☐ GOAL 5 ☐

Manifest That Shit!

November TO DO LIST ✓

WEEK 3:

_____

_____

_____

_____

_____

_____

_____

_____

_____

End of week **checkoff**! *How much did I accomplish this week?*

GOAL 1 ☐ GOAL 2 ☐ GOAL 3 ☐ GOAL 4 ☐ GOAL 5 ☐

WEEK 4:

_____

_____

_____

_____

_____

_____

_____

_____

_____

End of week **checkoff**! *How much did I accomplish this week?*

GOAL 1 ☐ GOAL 2 ☐ GOAL 3 ☐ GOAL 4 ☐ GOAL 5 ☐

December TO DO LIST ✓

WEEK 1:

_____

_____

_____

_____

_____

_____

_____

_____

*End of week **checkoff**! How much did I accomplish this week?*

GOAL 1 ☐ GOAL 2 ☐ GOAL 3 ☐ GOAL 4 ☐ GOAL 5 ☐

WEEK 2:

_____

_____

_____

_____

_____

_____

_____

_____

*End of week **checkoff**! How much did I accomplish this week?*

GOAL 1 ☐ GOAL 2 ☐ GOAL 3 ☐ GOAL 4 ☐ GOAL 5 ☐

Manifest That Shit!

December TO DO LIST ✓

WEEK 3:

_____
_____
_____
_____
_____
_____
_____
_____
_____
_____

End of week **checkoff!** *How much did I accomplish this week?*

GOAL 1 ☐ GOAL 2 ☐ GOAL 3 ☐ GOAL 4 ☐ GOAL 5 ☐

WEEK 4:

_____
_____
_____
_____
_____
_____
_____
_____
_____
_____

End of week **checkoff!** *How much did I accomplish this week?*

GOAL 1 ☐ GOAL 2 ☐ GOAL 3 ☐ GOAL 4 ☐ GOAL 5 ☐

Affirmations

Affirmations

Manifest That Shit!

Affirmations

Affirmations

Affirmations

Manifest That Shit!

Affirmations

Affirmations

Affirmations

Manifest That Shit!

Affirmations

Affirmations

Manifest That Shit!

Affirmations

Affirmations

People and products that can help you on your journey.

@TheSixFigureAuthor

@SweetCookieWash

@QueendomDinasty

@PowafulSex

@DarealbbJudy

@RushEscape

@StarrDawkinz

These pages will provide you with techniques,
tools, inspiration, and motivation to help you accomplish
a business, book, travel goal, and expose you to new amazing
products!

Thank you!